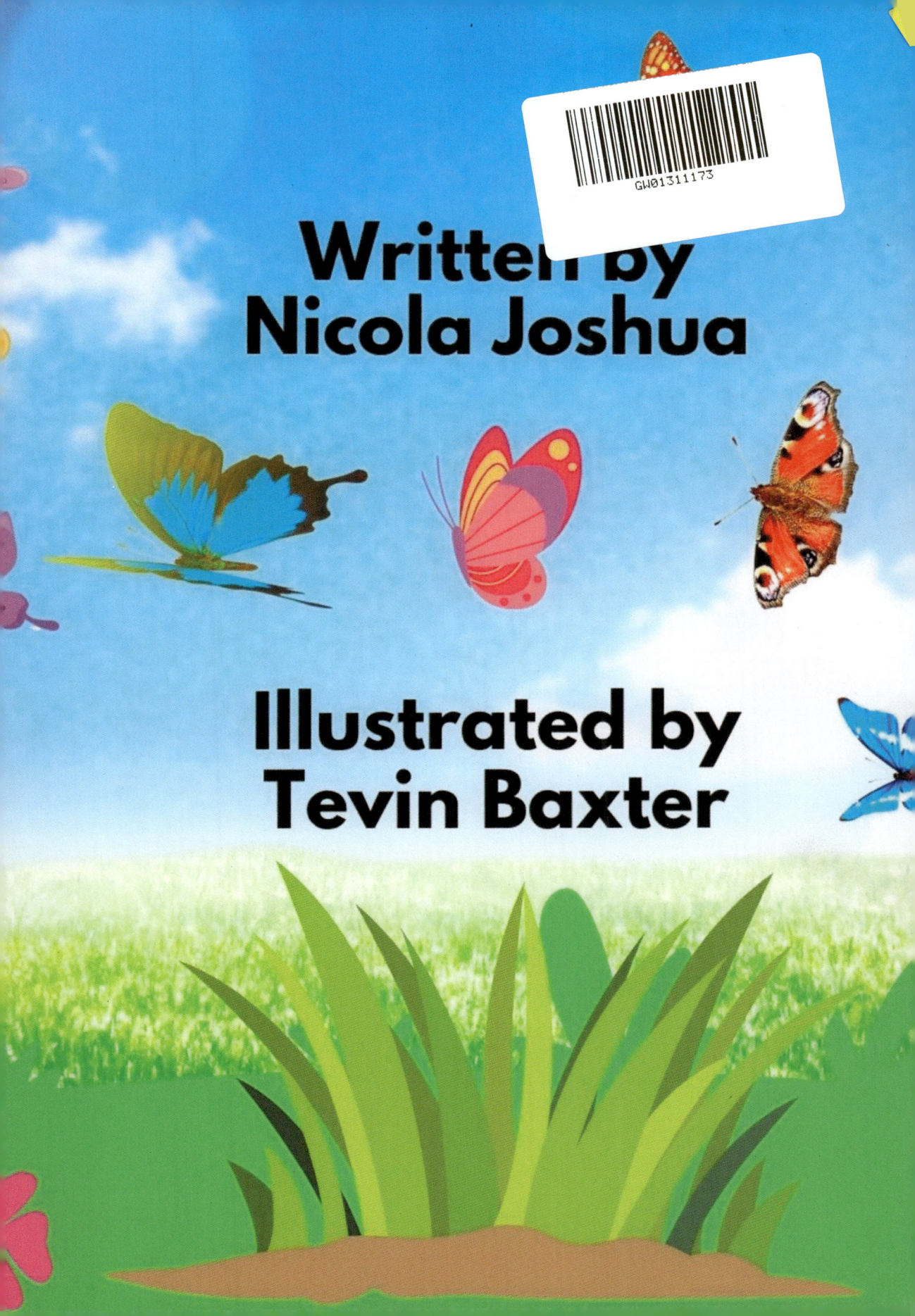

Written by
Nicola Joshua

Illustrated by
Tevin Baxter

Brown as I am on a hot June day.

Brown as I am
as I dream and
play.

Brown as I am,
I'm exploring
the world
with all its wonder.

Brown as I am
as I leap into
blue waters.

Brown as I am
and graceful as
I can be.

See how I twirl around this old oak tree.

Brown as I am, I can hop like a bunny.

Brown as I am
as I taste the
sweet honey.

**Brown as I am,
this skin is one
part of me.**

Brown as I am
that the world
can see.

Brown as I am,
I will make
my own way.

Brown as I am
and carefree
as I can be.

As I sit among the flowers during a warm summer breeze.

Please remember to leave a review our family will appreciate you.

More books to read!

You Are Loved: Coloring and Affirmation Book

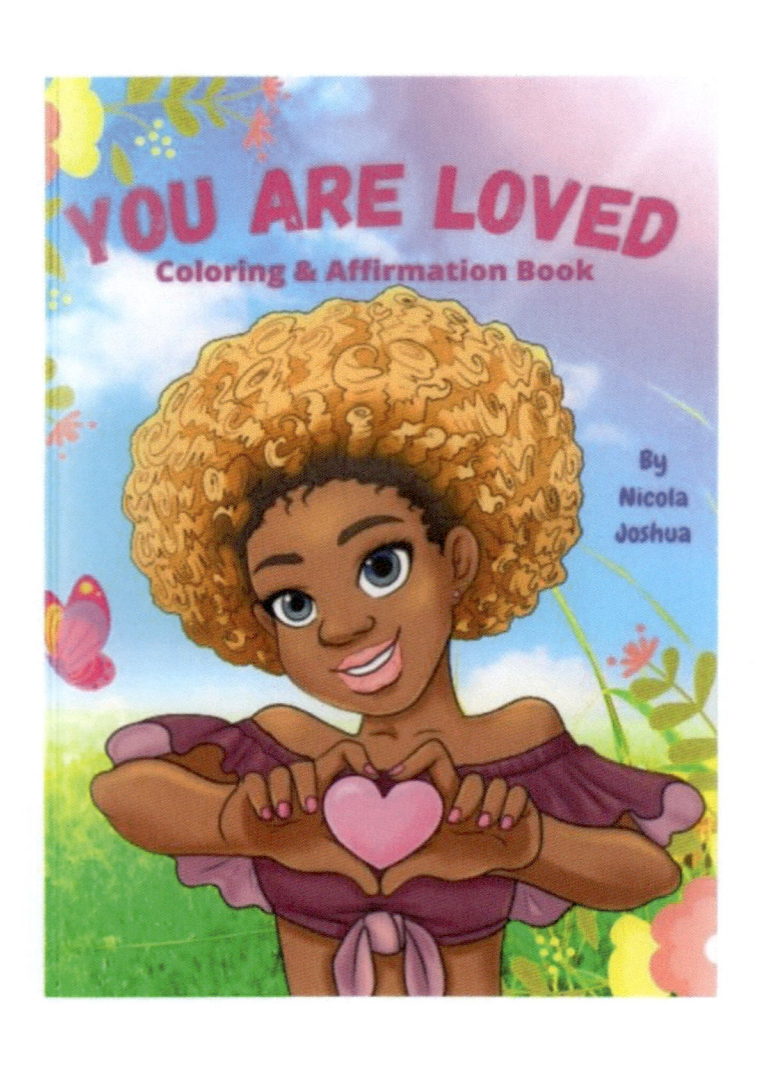

Brown As I Am: Empowering Boys in a Changing World

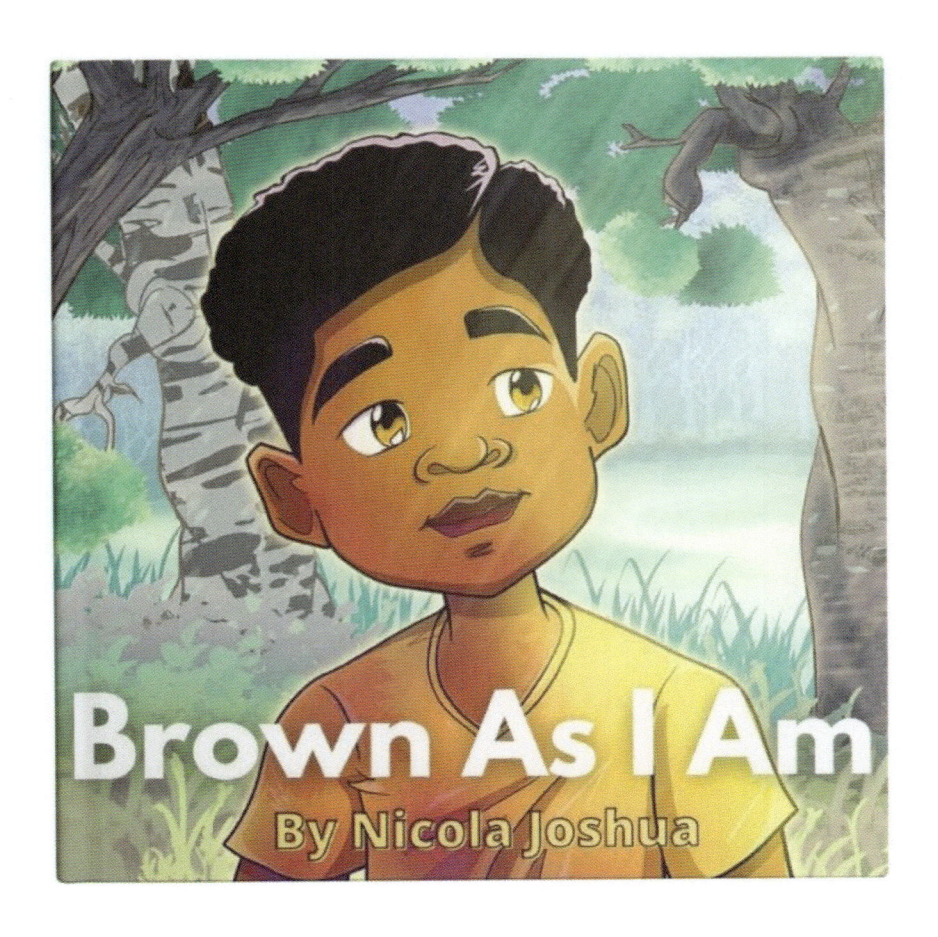

Printed in Great Britain
by Amazon